MW01231595

DARK PSYCHOLOGY OF PERSUASION

Understand the concept of persuasion, know how to apply it and discover the best techniques to convince others of unimportant facts, influence them and gain their trust.

Jason Smith

TABLE OF CONTENT

CHAPTER ONE

INTRODUCTION

Persuasion, either consciously or unconsciously, is a day to day practice that involves the use of a shared system of communication to influence a person, group, or organisation to take up an idea, belief, action or behaviour. At home, school, market or workplace, we attempt to convince people that a cause of action should be embraced while others should be abandoned without feeling too authoritative. Try to visualise a scenario where Adamo's parents ground him from playing video games. He then goes to the shelf, presents a scientific journal that claims video games help boys to relax better after engaging in long hours of studies. What he has done is simply to persuade his parents without pressing his opinion on them. The focus of the subsequent sections will be the scope of persuasion, types of persuasion, strategies of persuasion, stages of persuasion and aspects of persuasion.

WHAT IS PERSUASION?

Historically, persuasion is rooted in ancient Greek's model of a prised politician and orator.

To make the list, a politician or orator needs to master the use of rhetoric and elocution in other to persuade the public. Rhetoric, according to Aristotle, is the "ability to make use of the available methods of persuasion" in order to win a court case or influence the public during important orations. On the other hand, elocution (a branch of rhetoric), is the art of speech delivery which may include proper diction, proper gestures, stance and dress. Although Grecian politics and orations seem clearly to be the genesis of persuasion, its use in the rapidly developing world of the twenty-first century goes beyond politics, oration and other human endeavours.

Persuasion, in the business domain, refers to a corporate system of influence aimed at changing another people, groups, or organisations' attitude, behaviour or perception about an idea, object, goods, services or people. It often employs verbal communications (both written and spoken words), non-verbal communication (paralinguistic, chronemics, proxemics and so on), visual communication or a multimodal communication in order to convey, change or reinforce a piece of existing information or reasoning peculiar to the audience. Persuasion in business can come in different forms depending on the need of the management. For instance, business enterprise sometimes uses persuasion in cases like; public relations, broadcast, media relations, speech writing, social media, customer-client relations, employee communication, brand management and so on.

Persuasion, in psychological parlance, refers to the use of an obtainable understanding of the social, behavioural, or cognitive principles in psychology to influence the attitude, cognition, behaviour or belief system of a person, group or organisation. It is also seen as a process by which the attitude and behaviour of a person are influenced without any form of coercion but through the simple means of communication. For instance, when a child begs his mother for candy and the mother refuses but instead proffers a better food for the child to eat while also encouraging him that it will make him grow bigger. The child gets excited and goes for the new alternative. In this way, the mother has been able to tap into his belief system without any form of duress. Hence, persuasion can also be used as a method of social control.

In the world of politics and governing today, persuasion still retains its role as one of the important means of influencing the behaviour, feelings and commitment of the populace through the power of mass media. For instance, politicians sometimes use social media, television, radio, newspaper, magazine to persuade the populace to sponsor their political campaigns. Persuasion in modern politics is also observed through the use of authority in such situations where opponents of one political party influence on cross carpet to the other party with different promises in the form of power and immunity. In addition, the court still entertains the use of persuasion during the prosecution or defence of an accused.

Another way to see persuasion is through the intentional use of the means of communication as a tool of conviction to change attitudes regarding an issue by transferring messages in a free choice atmosphere. The verbal, non-verbal and visual forms of communication are manipulated just for the sole purpose of persuading an individual, group, or organisation. Although communication is the most important and versatile form in which persuasion is manifested, it is worthy of note

9

that not all forms of communication are intended to persuade. For instance, the celebration of a newly inaugurated president or governor circulated on the news cannot be classified as persuasion unless it is intended to impact something on the citizen of the country or react in certain ways.

We go further to look at other possible definition of persuasion in the circular world.

Persuasion is a concept of influence that attempts to change a person's attitudes, intentions, motivations, beliefs or behaviours. When a child begs his parent for candy and the parent says a big no to him, but the child insists on having candy even while knowing it might not be good for his health, persuasion is beginning to take place. Along the course of all of this, the parent will try to proffer a better food for the child to eat instead of the candy, the child gets excited and goes for the new alternative. In this way, the parent has won a banter of persuasion.

Persuasion on its own is a branch of communication and also popular as a method of social control, so it is worthy of note that not all forms of communication intend to be persuasive. Persuasion is also a process by which the attitude and behaviours of a person are influenced without any harsh treatments by simple means of communication from other people. Other factors can also determine a person's change in behaviour or attitude, for example, verbal threats, a person's current psychological state, physical coercion etc.

Persuasion can also be interpreted as using one's personal or positional resources to change people's behaviours or attitudes by using written or spoken words to pass across the information, feelings or reasoning or a combination of them. Another way to see persuasion is as a symbolic process in which people who communicate use tools of conviction to change attitudes regarding an issue through transferring of messages in a free choice atmosphere. In business, persuasion can be seen as an act of presenting a topic of argument to motivate, move or convince the audience. Persuasion is also used in presentations.

Having discussed the meanings of persuasion, it can be observed that persuasion extends beyond a specific field as there are an intermingling of ideas from different areas of study. However, communication and psychology seem clearly to be in use in order for persuasion to take place. While communication provides the model as to how interlocutors in the art of persuasion get messages understood, psychology provides the model for the mental processes during persuasion. Thus, communication and psychology and its use in persuasion will be the focus of the discussion in the upcoming chapter bur first; we will go on to debate the types of persuasion.

WHERE CAN PERSUASION BE USED

Where can persuasion be used?

In most cases, persuasion is used for personal gain and for a person's own means. In interpretation, persuasion can be seen as the use of a person's resource or political position to influence the decisions or behaviours of others. Over the years, persuasion has been used by many different people and in different places. At home, the mothers try to use persuasion to tweak the decisions of the father. The kids as seen in the example above try to change the decisions of their parents. At work, the workers might try to use persuasion to win the bosses over and the company in general uses persuasion to get a contract for themselves. The politicians try to make use of persuasion to drive home votes from the proletariat. At the market hub, there is usually the use of advertisement to dry to persuade potential customers to buy a certain product. Conversely, the buyer might not be satisfied with the price and might try to persuade the seller to bring down the price.

In general, persuasion has been said here to be available to anyone who can understand how it works and bank on it. Many times, people have won others over by understanding how it works.

So where can we use it

- Persuasion can be used at home
- Persuasion can be used to make friends
- Persuasion can be used to get a favour from friends and colleagues
- Persuasion can be used to influence anybody's decision
- Persuasion can be used in business to win contracts
- Persuasion can be a good tool to get jobs and be favoured at an interview

TYPE OF PERSUASION

This division is based on Shelly Chaiken's communication model that attempts to explain how people comprehend persuasive messages. The idea is that individuals can be persuaded in three major ways based on the method of reception and processing of persuasive messages. Hence, they can be persuaded; heuristically, systematically or through the combination thereof.

Heuristic persuasion: This is the type of persuasion in which the attitudes, behaviour, perception or beliefs of the audience are exploited with verbal, non-verbal or visual communications that appeals to the habit, imagination, feelings or emotion of the audience.

Heuristic persuasion uses judgmental rules known as knowledge structures that are learned and stored in the audience's memory, to achieve the goal of persuasion. It is governed by three principles; availability, accessibility, and applicability. Availability here simply refers to the ability of the persuader to use the knowledge structure that has been stored in the audience's memory. Accessibility refers to the ability of the persuader to induce the audience to retrieve the memory during persuasion. Applicability refers to the ability of the persuader to show the audience the relevance of the memory to the task of persuasion.

It is important to note that heuristic persuader usually uses his position as an expert or uses information that is endorsed by other authorities in order to persuade the audience that does not fully process the semantic content of the information presented to them or if the information does not affect them (audience) personally.

Systematic persuasion: This is the type of persuasion in which attitudes, behaviour, perception or beliefs of the audience are influenced through the exhaustive means of logic and reasoning. It can also be a form of persuasion in which the persuader uses a step-by-step or cause-effect method to present relevant information in order to influence the audience's attitudes, behaviour or perception.

Systematic persuasion uses valuable sources and information that are reliable and available to the audience to make a stronger impact on their comprehension during the persuasion task. In the process of performing the task, the persuader relies heavily on the audience's thorough treatment of the relevant information and how they (audience) respond accordingly to the semantic content of the message being relayed to them. Systematic persuasion influences the audience's mental efforts significantly by actively allowing them (audience) to comprehend, evaluate and respond to the message's content. During the systematic process of persuasion, the persuader also makes sure that the audience can assess the validity of the statement as it relates to the message's conclusion.

Systematic persuader encourages the persuader to break down the information into steps that can be understood and explains the purpose of the information in order to produce the desired change in attitude, behaviour or opinion. Hence, it should be noted that although systematic persuasion depends heavily on the persuader's ability to present the information and classify the sources correctly, relevant visual contents can also be used to support the audience's assessment of validity in the persuasive message.

Heuristic-systematic persuasion: This is the borderline between heuristic and systematic type of persuasion. In this type of persuasion, the attitudes, behaviour, perception or beliefs of the audience are influenced through the combinatory use of logic, reasoning, imagination, emotion, feelings and so on.

Heuristic-systematic persuasion is premised on the hypothesis that neither heuristic nor a systematic type of persuasion is efficient on its own except that the two are combined to achieve the goal of persuasion. When any one of the above (heuristic or systematic persuasion) is used alone, there are possibilities that it will be unstable, and the behaviour, emotion and feelings of the audience will become unpredicted. This is because credibility and source of information determine the success of persuasion if the audience is involved or required to give a response. Heuristic-systematic persuader should, therefore, alternate between Heuristic and systematic persuasion so that the audience can have the choice of accepting the credibility and source of information which they would have otherwise rejected.

Consequently, the heuristic-systematic persuader should take cognizance of the circumstances surrounding the persuasion in order to determine the type of persuasion to be used and when to switch in case the other seems to be failing.

METHODS OF PERSUASION

People make use of persuasion for different reasons and the ways they use to get what they want from others also differs. In this section, we will be looking at the ways in which persuasion can be is achieved. How people persuade and what studies have been made to back these methods. The methods of persuasion can also be termed as the modes or strategies or devices that can be used to classify the speakers appeal to the audience.

In a discourse, however, persuasion can be achieved in three different ways,

When a speaker speech is so well structured and spoken and the hearers are compelled to believe in what he says and accept it totally

Persuasion can also be achieved when the hearers buy into the idea of the speaker because what he has spoken about has caught their attention.

It can also be achieved through the speech itself. When the speaker has laid down an argument and the audience believe that the speech has proven a truth or has opened their eyes to a new cause or phenomenon.

In this book though, we want to look at methods that can be used in day to day life to seek to persuade people.

A. THE FOOT IN THE DOOR METHOD

The major principle of this method is to ask for big favour but before doing that, one would need to ask for a smaller favour first. By asking for something smaller, the one who is being asked favour will not find it hard to grant a request. He will fill committed to what you have asked initially and when the big bomb comes, he will already be into it to tell you a no. It will be like a continuation of favour which he had already agreed on. There are some real-life situations that one can apply the use of this persuasive method in.

For example, if you fail a test and you want a retake, it might not be advisable to go to the lecturer to request foe a direct retake of the exam, instead, why not first ask the lecturer for a feedback or a follow up to the reason why you have failed the examination. After he has given a feedback, you can then go forward to ask for a retake. It is paramount to add that then trying to make use of this method of persuasion, one should tread carefully and not rush into asking for the favour.

B. DOOR IN THE FACE METHOD

This is the direct opposite of the method mentioned above. What is needed here is to first ask for a big favour before asking for a smaller one. So how is this supposed to work? It's simple, the first question is meant to let the person you're requesting something from say no, then if not that then you put in the next request. Okay, to a real example of how it truly works. If I asked, I wrote you an article and said, would you rather scream around your neighbourhood naked speaking about how awesome it is? You'd say no right? Then I go on to say, why not read and share the article instead. You see, you'd definitely go for this option. A real-life situation is requesting for a loan of $500 from your friend and when he says he can't, you can go down to ask for a $50 loan. Now it's not that hard, is it?

C. THE ANCHORING METHOD

This is a technique used mostly for the pricing of goods. Anchoring is a type of cognitive decision making based on things that are present. For you to know which product is ideal, you, first of all, take another product that is probably similar or closely similar in value and use and compare the two products. From here, you can go on to decide which product is the best for you. If this method is properly used, it can really stir a person's business into so much success.

For example. As business owner, you have a car put up for sale put up for sale and a customer comes in, the initial value of the car including the profit takes it up to 7000 but you tell the customer that it is 10000 and the customer brings it all down to 8000, and you agree, this way the customer is really satisfied with his purchase and you have made more progress in yours too. The initial asking price of 10000 is serving here as an anchor as the customer will see any price below it as a very good deal. The customer goes home satisfied and you too can go home making a good profit.

D. COMMITMENT AND CONSISTENCY METHOD

Humans have been known to be consistent in their actions in life and therefore this is one of the strongest of these methods written here. Commitment and consistency have to do with using a person's already known love for something to your own means. This way, the person will only be helping you based on their love for what you need help for. It wouldn't be anything compulsory because the person will, in fact, enjoy doing what you want. In a real-life situation, you could ask a person if they like the environment and want the environment to be very good in the next few years. When they answer in the positive, you can then go further to ask them to join an eco-friendly group of people who seek to put up an awareness about the environment. They instantly become committed and go on to become the best member of that group. Okay, to you, you can ask yourself, why do you keep buying that brand every time, why do you keep using iPhone every single time a new model is released. This is because you feel a commitment to it and as such you are consistent to that brand. Another relatable example is that one has about how having a goal can lead to productivity. One thing that is very popular about this is the use of a self-help book. The reason why the use of a book like this is effective is because of one's commitment to what is written there and it ultimately leads to consistency because you know that this is what you want and you will most definitely stick to it especially when those things are written down.

E. SOCIAL GROUP METHOD

This is a very noticeable persuasion technique and I believe everyone has done this at a time or the other. This method is based practically on the decisions of others. You are persuaded to do things because other people also do it. You take part in a task because others also take part in it. When in a social gathering, and a friend comes up with an idea, everyone instantly goes to that idea even though they do not agree to it. One real-life instance is a research that states that most people will like a Facebook post that has many likes than one with zero likes. This method states that most people look at what their peers do and what action they take and react based on that action. People take to smoking due to social proof. Many people smoke so why not, I too should smoke despite all the obvious health hazards and the not so good taste.

F. AUTHORITY METHOD

This is one of the very good ways in business to get customers. It is based on telling people that your business has been listed or recommended by a higher authority. This way, people will definitely want to buy it.

This method is not only applicable in business but also in other aspects of life. People look up to authority in many different fields and different areas of life. So, making yourself a source of authority can persuade people to work with you and it can, in turn, take you a long way. An example in business is when a lesser company or a start-up, for example, uses "as seen on" on their landing pages especially when this type of websites has been featured or probably recommended by other major websites. Another great example is when an agency mentions the name of their big previous clients on their websites especially if they have really worked with big companies so as to make people believe and trust the credibility of the service they are going to render.

G. SCARCITY METHOD

This is another method used by many businesses especially online businesses. With the scarcity method, it is very possible for one to win the hearts of customers over. This technique is done by telling those who intend to buy from you that the product is about to finish, or the offer will last for a period. This way, the customers will not want to miss out on that offer and will prefer to grab it immediately. This is a very good way to get people to buy things from you. They will see it now as an opportunity to buy the product. You will not have to do so much convincing as opposed to some other methods up here. I think it is safe to say that this is the easiest of these methods, but the offer should be very eye catchy and mouth watery for them to be interested in it initially.

Overall, the major basis of this work is limited time and limited or limited supply. An example of the use of this method is when a popular website booking.com always talks about how there are only 2 or 3 rooms left in the hotel or how about 20 other people that are also searching for that same hotel. This way, more people will want to get the room since it is a possibility that others might get the room before them.

This technique is very popular amongst door to door salesmen that go around and say they are doing a special that will only last a day and once they're gone, they are never to be seen again. Finally, we might be surfing the internet and then we see an advert saying, THIS IS GOING TO CHANGE YOUR LIFE FOREVER, BUY NOW BEFORE IT IS TAKEN DOWN, apparently, everyone would want their lives to be changed so they'll want to go for it. The technique is more popularly used by scammers now but if used appropriately, one can use it to make sales.

H. RECIPROCATION METHOD

This is a very good technique in the sense that many people feel obliged to pay back a favour and so that is why this technique is a very effective one. The method is used by giving favour either big or small to a person and then requesting what it is you want in return. Through that which you have done, the person will feel indebted to you. And you will have a greater chance of getting something back. As the popular saying goes, "I owe you one", so here, there is a debt to be repaid.

A good life example is when you are organizing a good orphan donation and instead of just asking for donations straight away, you instead start by telling the kids to help make some very good bracelets or necklaces for the donors and at the beginning, you start by sharing the bracelets, the donors will feel indebted and will readily make their donations. Also, when reading an article online, it is also very evident that the writers after helping to solve a problem or have thought a lesson requests that you share at the end. If you have ever hit that share button or that like button, it is because of the fact that article or probably that YouTube video has added some value to you.

I. FRAMING METHOD

Framing is a technique that is popularly used by politicians or those who are into a debate and is used to try to win the hearts of those that are listening. Framing is done by carefully explaining a certain point in a way that the recipient is convinced and can agree with a speaker. The recipient should be able to interpret the information in your own desired way.

A good example is the classic example of a half full glass cup and a half empty glass cup. This phrase sounds much more positive meanwhile it can be interpreted otherwise depending on how the speaker wans the hearer to see his point from. As stated earlier, this method is popularly used by politicians who are looking to beat their opponents in a debate by making the audience see their point of view.

Framing has some elements that are used when being used and they are aptly discussed below.

Choosing the right people, time and place to communicate.

Approach- carefully choosing the right words to use to communicate. By explaining the positives of your point, people are likely to get more convinced than when one speaks about the downside.

Words- by selecting the most suitable words to use when communicating.

J. LOSS AVERSION

This is based on cognitive biases and it was discovered based on a psychology research by Daniel Kahneman and Amos Tversky. The concept of loss aversion state that more people will go for a programme if the possibility of loss is quite reduced compared to another. The propounds of these methods brought a specific illustration to back their theory.

If the United States was preparing for a certain outbreak of a disease and it is expected to kill a number of about 600 people and there is a certain alternative to the problem by saying that if programme A is adopted, then 300 people will be saved and if programme B is followed then there is a 1/3 that 600 people will be saved and 2/3 probability that if the programme is carried out, nobody will be saved, then more people will opt to go for the first programme because the risk levels are very low as opposed to the second programme where people can die based on probability.

In businesses, a company can come up with an idea to deal with a certain problem by fist giving two or more alternatives. One or more alternatives with a higher risk possibility and one with a low risk which in most cases will be chosen by the customer.

K. THE BECAUSE METHOD

This is another day to day method that is very effective when used appropriately. There is not so much explanation to this method. You can use this to win favour, get people to do what you want and to also listen to you. It works simply by telling these people the actual reason why you'll be needing them to do a certain thing for you.

For example, when you meet a person on a line probably where you are about to get a ticket or where you want to buy a food but you need to get what you want pretty fast and you ask like this "can I jump the line at your front?" you might be allowed to stay there probably because you're cute or maybe because of the weird way you asked but in most cases, the recipient will instantly start looking for ways to decline your request. Instead of making such request like that, why not say. "Can I jump the line I in front of you because I have not eaten since yesterday and I need to take a medication or because I would be late for work". This way, your chances of getting what you want can be fulfilled by just saying the reason why you want what you want. The word because is very powerful, make sure to use it in your communication and see how it helps you get what you want yourself.

CHAPTER 2

In the first chapter, we have been able to develop on what persuasion is, we extensively defined the concept in different aspects of life. We then went on to tell where it can be used. Types of persuasion were then discussed and finally the methods by which one can use persuasion. We agreed that it is a broad concept and can be used in different means. As we go forward, we will be looking at the strategies of analysing persuasion and then move on to the stages of persuasion and also the aspects of persuasion.

STRATEGIES OF PERSUASION

Strategies of persuasion refer to the techniques, tactics or procedure of achieving persuasion, whether at home, in the office, during political rallies, during court trials and so on. It was first introduced by Aristotle who describes it as an act of showing someone how something is used or done. He believes that people are fully persuaded when they considered the thing well demonstrated. These methods are still relevant to the art of persuasion today and they include;

- **Ethos**: This is the distinguishing character, sentiment, moral nature or guiding beliefs of a person, group or organisation. It refers to the ability of the persuader to prove the credibility of the discussion in the process of convincing the audience. This can be as a result of the persuader being an authority, have demonstrated the mastery of the terminology used in the field or has ьeen introduced by an established authority. For instance, a doctor has the capability to influence the choice of chemotherapy and physiotherapy regarding a cancer patient because he is seen as knowledgeable in the field.

- **Pathos**: This is an element in experience or in artistic representation evoking pity or compassion. It refers to the ability of the persuader to solicit the audience emotion or feelings by telling or showing stories or expressions that alights with the underlying values, beliefs or attitude of the audience. This can be done by using troops or figures of speech (e.g. metaphor, simile, personification, litotes and so on) that appeals to the audience's imagination, thereby provoking hope, optimism and other forms of positivity. Example of this can be found in speeches by politicians, political activists, motivational speakers and so on.

- **Logos**: It refers to the ability of the persuader to use logic to appeal to the audience's knowledge of facts and figures or cause and effect. The persuader relies heavily on the ethos to realise or achieve the aim. For instance, a teacher can persuade a student having problems in economics to take a mathematics course with the claim that those who took the course (mathematics) in the past performed excellently well in economics. Here, the teacher is using facts and figures to persuade the student.

- **Kairos**: This is the ability of the persuader to use the setting of the stage or environment to persuade the audience. It involves the ability to use the happenings around (i.e. place and time) to push forward his claims. For instance, advertisements are placed on Facebook to persuade people to take cyber security courses in order to protect their computers from malicious hackers. This can be observed as a result of the changing meaning of security as reflected in the transition into the technological age.

type of persuasion is a conscious process which
:s different stages. The purpose of the stages is to
the audience through the phase in such a manner
∠ will make them (audience) accept the change in
naviour or attitude and simultaneously, act. Different
tages have been proffered regarding persuasion.

However, William McGuire's model for the stages in persuasion has been selected because of its relevance to the ongoing discussion. According to McGuire, there are six stages in persuasion namely; presentation, awareness, comprehension, acceptance, retention and action.

Subsequently, each stage will be explained in detail, citing examples from our day to day activities.

- **Presentation**: This refers to the persuasive message per se and the means that have been adopted to reach the targeted audience.
  For instance, a student, who wants to persuade his lecturer for a retake of test or examination that he had performed woefully in, will be careful not to write a letter or call the lecture at an odd hour in the day when he can see the lecturer in person. Hence, the persuader should determine beforehand what type of persuasion and form of communication will be effective and expressive in such a situation.

- **Awareness**: This is the most technical stage of the six stages of persuasion as persuaders often repeat it on countless times until they hit the bull's eyes. At this point, the persuader is ready to relay the message to the audience but first, he/she has to create the necessary impression that the message is worth listening to by using any of the psychological principles of persuasion (to be explained under persuasion and psychology) proposed by Cialdini.

Take for instance the student who wanted to ask for a retake in a test. He knocks on the lecturer's office and goes in but to his utmost surprise, the lecturer sends him out without giving him the chance to express himself. You might ask if there's something wrong with this approach? It could be that he has not made any formal appointment with the lecturer or he did not wait for the lecturer's order to enter. Hence, the persuader must be careful not to jeopardize the task of persuasion during the stage of awareness.

- **Comprehension**: This is the stage where the persuader confirms if the audience really understood the message that is being communicated to them. The persuader is usually advised to avoid any form of ambiguity during verbal and non-verbal communication. The persuader should also avoid overburdening the audience with any form of information that is not relevant to the discussion during persuasion. The persuader can confirm verbally by asking simple questions like; 'do you understand?', 'shall we proceed to the next step?' and so on.

Whenever question crops up from the audience, the persuader should answer in a polite way that will not make the audience feel threatened. If the persuader must take a turn in asking questions, he should do it one at a time.

- **Acceptance**: This stage involves getting the audience to say 'yes, I agree with your point of view'. The persuader should use all possible means that will make the audience trust in the above-mentioned process without leaving any iota of doubt in them. For instance, if you offer the lowest price regarding a standard product, should people be sceptical? On the other hand, if you offer the highest price, have you been able to convince the audience that what you are providing is the best of the best? This is because we trust people/brands that make us trust them though there are other brands that can provide the same services. Hence, trust is important for the acceptance stage to be completed.

- **Retention**: This stage requires that you consolidate the above-mentioned process by reiterating them using media like social media, radio commercials, and advertisement.

For instance, companies of reputable names do employ social media savvies who are current with the happenings in the society and who can use such a situation to persuade the audience. In this sense, they keep tabs with the audience that they have been able to convince.

- **Action**: We want people to act from our persuasive message by responding to us, seeing us, listening to us or buy from us. For instance, traditional media like radio commercial gives a short period of time to get the persuasive message out which is a non-visual message and thus, relying upon their ears to provide the attention.

However, with television, we have the audio-visual where the audience can listen and see at the same time.

In social media, more options are even available where the audience can respond immediately to the persuasive message.

ASPECTS OF PERSUASION

In most cases, persuasion is used for personal gain and for a person's own means. In interpretation, persuasion be the use of a person's resource or political position to influence the decisions or behaviours of others. Over the years, persuasion has been used by many different people and in different places.

At home, the mothers try to use persuasion to influence the decisions of the father. The kids as seen in the example above try to change the decisions of their parents.

At work, the workers might try to use persuasion to win the bosses over and the company in general uses persuasion to get a contract for themselves. The politicians try to make use of persuasion to drive home votes from the proletariat.

At the market hub, there is usually the use of advertisement to persuade potential customers to buy a certain product. Conversely, the buyer might not be satisfied with the price and might try to persuade the seller to bring down the price.

In general, persuasion has been said to be available to anyone who can understand how it works and bank on it.

Many times, people have won others over by understanding how it works. So where can we use it

Persuasion can be used at home: This can be used by any member of the family to gain their kids' or spouses' attention and make them take actions.

Imagine a situation whereby the husband needs to be intimate with his wife, there is a need to persuade her with pleasing words. If not, it will be regarded as rape.

Persuasion can be used to make friends: It is also used to gain friends. In fact, studies have found out that people who make a lot of friends both in-person or other means like social media have an efficient method of persuasion. This should, however, be distinguished from peer pressure. While persuasion is non-coercive, peer pressure is forceful as the name suggest.

Persuasion can be used to influence anybody's decision: Many times in real-life encounters, you will hear people say, 'you see that guy over there, he is very stingy but only God knows how Tolu manage to borrow things from him without squeezing his face'. Some will even tag it as a code but in sooth, these persuaders have mastered and successfully practised it.

Persuasion can be used in business to win contracts: Although, it is used mostly in the business organisations to win contracts, other use like; public relations, broadcast, media relations, speech writing, social media, customer-client relations, employee communication, brand management and so on. Hence, the business organisation serves as the most used avenue by persuaders.

Persuasion can be a good tool to get jobs and be favoured at an interview: In the changing world of the job application, the job seeker must be able to persuade the organisation or company that he or she is capable of maintaining the vacant position that is being advertised. While it is much easier with interviews, the persuader employs extra effort during written letters like recommendation letter because any misuse of words cannot be corrected again after it has been submitted.

CHAPTER 3

PERSUASION, COMMUNICATION AND BUSINESS

Aristotle has stressed the importance of rhetoric and elocution in the art of persuasion. However, the introduction of new methods of information and communication technology has reshaped our thinking about communication as a means of persuasion. This is because it is one of the fast-growing and easiest methods of persuasion available at home, in the office, and even in the market.

Persuasion, in most instances, uses communication to achieve its aim by exploiting all the means of communication, both verbal, non-verbal and visual available to humans though it is been stressed that not all forms communications are persuasive. Some focus on enhancing social relationship while others are merely for record-keeping.

What is communication? What are the strategies of communication used in persuasion?

How does persuasion work in a business setting? Thus, this chapter will strive to demystify the above questions in the succeeding sections.

WHAT IS COMMUNICATION?

Communication is one of the unifying forces that bind human beings from diverse spheres of life together. Without it, man is thought to share no significant difference with the animals that roam the forest. Can you imagine a classroom, business, market or congress where they lack a common system of communication? Such an organization will be haphazardly maintained and the purpose of setting it up will be defeated. This is the reason communication is given preference in any chosen endeavour by man. Although we can argue that animals have their own system of communication, they are not accessible to different species other than their kind.

Communication, in its cultural sense, refers to the exchange of ideas, messages, feelings or thoughts using comprehensible channel (verbal, non-verbal or visual) between two people, groups or organizations who share the same understanding. From the definition, it can be deduced that certain requirements need to be met for communication to take place.

They include (1) Sender/encoder (2) encoding (3) message/code (4) Channel/medium (5) Receiver/decoder (6) decoding and (7) Feedback. The sender initiates the communication process by sending messages across to the receiver using a culturally accepted manner of transmission in the form of signs, sounds or body language. The receiver decodes the messages by reassembling them to his/her individual linguistic ability and for communication to reach its final stage, the receiver must be able to give replies and expect feedbacks in return.

There are three major forms of communication namely:

- Verbal
- Non-Verbal
- Visual communication.

Verbal communication refers to the exchange of oral and written words between two correspondents who share the same understanding about an idea, feeling or belief. Conversely, non-verbal communication is the absence of spoken or written words in the transmission of information between two parties that share the same understanding about an idea, feeling or belief.

Examples of non-verbal communicate include paralinguistic, proxemics, chronemics and kinesics. Visual communication refers to the interchange of ideas, feelings, and emotions between two correspondents in forms that are clearly visible to the eyes.

Non-verbal communication in persuasion refers to the use of body language, facial expression and other means apart from the use of spoken or written forms to influence to inspire changes in the audience's behaviours, perceptions or attitudes. It is also seen as the process of making others embrace or resist new attitudes and feelings with or without the accompaniment of verbal means of communication.

Many individuals impulsively associate persuasion with verbal information only though non-verbal communication also stresses the fact that verbal communication can be complemented by non-verbal communication in order to expatiate on the meaning of the information that is being passed across to the audience

Non-verbal communication in persuasion also examines the concept of social influence. Social influence focuses on the absence of words or linguistic choices that are used to bring about a particular influence level on the audience when getting involved in the act of stirring changes in behaviour or predetermined attitude. Non-verbal communication in persuasion includes appeals to attraction, similarity and intimacy.

Attraction: Attraction here simply refers to the personal attraction that exists within the persuader. It is a confident outlook that matches with the possibility of responding to a person with positive responses from another person, group or organisation. This is the reason it is regarded as a part of the three major classifications of stimuli that decide the realisation of persuasive efforts since it is a noticeable characteristic of the source of the information.

For instance, it has been discovered that information that comes from a beautiful person is believed to be more persuasive than information coming from normal looking or unattractive sources, a more reason why celebrities in the sport or movie arenas are selected to persuade the people either for business or political purpose.

However, the level of influence through attractiveness usually differs from one audience to another since persuasive power of attractiveness can even be contrary to intuition or common sense.

Moreover, attractiveness can be more persuasive than the credibility or logic behind an argument and the idea that the best type of argument is the most logical one is unnecessarily true when a contradictory argument is coming from a highly attractive person.

In addition, the persuader often pairs non-verbal communication with irregular persuasive tactics. This is realised by joining certain non-verbal communication with certain tactics that would bring about an advanced level of success in implementing change as long as they are coupled correctly.

For instance, when trying to persuade someone with the focus on preventing an idea, behaviour or attitude, it is better to employ a non-verbal style that is thoroughly considered (systematic). On the other hand, when trying to persuade someone with the focus on promoting an idea, behaviour or attitude, it is better to use a flexible or relaxed non-verbal style (heuristic).

In real life situation, the point of agreement between attraction and persuasion can be observed in the interactions between two people engaging in flirtation or dating. It has been noticed that at the beginning of a fresh relationship, the audience will focus more on preventing the idea of likeness or love and thus, the body language will reveal an effort to keep distance but it is up to the persuader to observe this and be careful about what other non-verbal tactics to be used. Nevertheless, when the two people (the persuader and the audience) are more relaxed and get more accustomed to each other, the focus then shifts from prevention to promotion. From this time, the persuader's body language, as well as other non-verbal clues, will change and equal the focus.

Similarity: Similarity here refers to the attitude, experience, values, communication styles or knowledge that the persuader has in common with the audience. It also denotes the non-verbal communication of behaviour, attitude or perception in persuasion in which the persuader suggests the similarity in feelings or opinions to the audience once they are not conferred openly. For instance, there is a high probability of an audience with an athletic interest to be persuaded by any sportsman because of the similar interest they share.

The concept of attraction and similarity is usually examined side by side since the non-verbal clues that suggest or connote the latter impressions also influence the former impressions. For instance, if the persuader notices what attracts the audience to him, he might make efforts to show the similarities that exist between him (the persuader) and the audience in order to influence their behaviour or attitude.

However, if the persuader shows non-verbal clues that cause the audience to infer that they do not share similar attitudes or beliefs, there will be less attraction.

Intimacy: Intimacy simply refers to the persuader's inherent drive to create a strong connection or link through a friendly interpersonal relationship. The persuader normally views the persuasive message as those which the audience can connect to on a personal level. However, it may be extremely difficult to influence a large and diverse audience during a non-verbal communication through the use of intimacy except if the audience is a small homogeneous group. Hence, attempts should be made to view intimacy from the audience's angle and where it can be used.

PARALINGUISTICS IN PERSUASION

Paralinguistic's simply refers to the non-verbal elements of speech, and to a limited extent of writing, used to modify meaning and convey an emotion such as pitch, volume and intonation. It is also seen as one of the many ways that depict non-verbal behaviour, attitude or opinion. Paralinguistic in persuasion is therefore carried out through the use of kinesics, proxemics, physical appearance, artefacts and chronemics.

Kinesics: This is a non-verbal communication by means of gestures, and/or other body movements. It is seen as a complex method in communication whereby the persuader uses, eye contact, body movement or facial expression to influence the attitude, belief or opinion of the audience. For instance, it has been noticed that in flirtation or dating, the persuader stares at the other party to connote infatuation or when verbal communication fails, while averting gaze is likely to show that the persuader is shy.

Proxemics: This is the study of the effect of the physical distance between people in different cultures and societies. In persuasion, it refers to the use of physical space to influence the attitude, belief or perception of the audience. The distance between the persuader and the audience in a social situation often determines or exposes information about the level of their relationship. Also, it can disclose the type of social setting going on.

For instance, the persuader's distance from lovers, children, close family members and friends, as well pet animals ranges to about 18 inches apart while the distance reserved for strangers, newly formed groups, and new acquaintances range from 4 to 8 feet away. Also, the distance used for speeches, lectures, and theatre includes anything more than 8 feet away. The knowledge of personal, social and public distance is therefore important when influencing the audience.

Physical Appearance and Artefacts: Physical appearance simply refers to the persuader's outlook or physical disposition while artefacts refer to the paraphernalia of influence used by the persuader. It has been observed that they (physical appearance and artefacts) can basically decide the persuasive effects and the credibility of the persuader, which in turn has a substantial impact on acceptance or refusal of the audience.

Physical appearance, clothing, status symbols an individual wear are often potent clues used by persuaders to influence the behaviour or attitude of the audience because they signify the ability and confidence of the persuader to socially influence through the above mention items.

Chronemics: This is usually associated with the perception that time is valuable. Often, we hear the adage "time is money" and thus, the persuader's use of this simple understanding is to influence the decision or opinion of the audience. The more important the persuader seems to be, the longer the amount of time the audience will want to spend with him.

It has been noticed that facial expression changes with time and the persuader, therefore, changes his facial expression to meet the need of the situation. For instance, human emotions communicate messages to show that they are happy, excited, sad, or moody and as such, the emotions vary significantly with time. Therefore, as the messages they communicate facially vary so should the persuaders.

However, facial expression coupled with the gestures of the persuader can communicate opposing messages depending on whether hand gestures are employed properly or paired with varying verbal or linguistic communication. For instance, if the gestures are not paired properly with the verbal approach being used to persuade a target audience, the success achieve with the message may be doubtful.

The use of gesture as a nonverbal cue in checking for behaviour is properly employed by the persuader; it can effect a change in behaviour or attitude which is the reason persuasion is employed in communication.

VISUAL COMMUNICATION IN PERSUASION

What is the best visual persuasion?

Visual communication in persuasion, from its name, simply refers to the ability to influence the attitude, belief, perception, opinion, or idea of an audience through the use of visual aids like; signs, typography, drawing, graphic design, illustration, industrial design, advertising, animation, colour, and electronic resources. Also, it refers to the actual representation of the information through a visible medium such as text or images that are aesthetically designed to entice the audience. The visual aids partially or holistically depend on the power of the persuader to make it appeal to the audience's sight. Hence, a good visual persuasion is usually assessed based on the persuader's success in increasing or decreasing the audience's comprehension of the information embedded in the visual aids.

Furthermore, recent trends in this form of persuasion have focused on web design and graphically oriented usability. Visual communication is perhaps the most important form of persuasion that takes place while users are surfing the Internet. When experiencing the web, the audience is then influenced through the use of visuals that appeals to their (audience) eyes, which is the primary sense of receiving visual information.

For instance, a visual persuader could be a graphic designer who uses excellent visual communication in their professional practise in order to

47

influence the populace. Therefore, the appropriate use of visual materials on a website is very important for the audience to understand and act upon the information that is being relayed to them.

Apart from the two-dimensional images commonly used as a means of visual communication, there are other ways to express ideas and persuade visually. I.e. the use of gestures and body language, animation (either digital or analogue) and film. Visual communication in persuasion also takes the form of e-mail or textual medium that is usually expressed through (American Standard Code for Information Interchange.) ASCII art, emoticons, and embedded digital images. Thus, visual persuasion has become one of the most important approaches to persuading people.

Visual communication takes place as a result of the use of graphs, charts and pictures, not just that, but also takes place through the use of signs and symbols. It may be used either independently or as an adjunct to the other methods of communication.

Image analysis

Visual communication contains image aspects. To be able to fully interpret images, one needs to be subjective. This is also needed to understand the full concept of meaning, or many meanings, communicated in an image requires analysis. Images can be analyzed through many perspectives, for example, these six major perspectives presented by Paul Martin Lester:

Personal perspective

When a person personally has a view about an image based on their own thoughts. This concept is dependent on the viewer's own thoughts and values, which is peculiar to the person. This might, however, be in conflict sometimes with cultural values. Also, it is hard to alternate the view of the image on the person who as viewed when a viewer has viewed that image with a personal perspective already, even though the image can also be viewed in other ways.

Historical perspective

An image's view can be arising from the history of the users' use of media. Through history, the sort of images has been changed, because of the use of different kinds of new media. For example, the use of the computer to edit images like Photoshop, CorelDraw and other editors will be quite different when comparing them with images that are made and edited using handmade craft.

Technical perspective

Technical perspective has to do with light. This is how the view of an image has been influenced through the use of lights or the presentation and the position of the image.

The correct use of light, position and presentation of an image can make better how the image is viewed. The image might not be good, but the light has changed that.

Ethical perspective

From the ethical perspective, the person who makes the image, the one who views it and the image must take responsibility for the moral and ethical aspects of the image. This perspective can be categorized into six separate parts: utilitarianism, imperative, golden mean, hedonism, golden rule and veil of ignorance.

Cultural perspective

The important definition for this perspective is symbolization. Cultural perspective involves the use of the identity of symbols. The uses of words that are totally related to the image, the use of heroes in the image, etc. These are the symbolization of the image. The cultural perspective can also be called the semiotic perspective.

Critical perspective

The view of this critical perspective is when the viewer criticizes the images, but the critics have been made in interests of the society, although an individual is the one that makes up the critics. This way this perspective is different from the personal perspective.

Visual aids

Visual aids are mostly used to help audiences of persuasive and informative speeches better understand the topic that is being presented. Visual aids play a large role in explaining how the audience can understand and take in all the information that is presented. There are different types of visual aids that spans from handouts to PowerPoint. The type of visual aid that a speaker decides to use will be dependent on their own preference and the kind of information they are looking to present.

Visual communication plays a very vital role in our day today life. Advertisement, teaching and learning, presentation and SEO and so on all involve visual communication to some extent.

Each type of visual aid its own advantages and disadvantages that must be well evaluated to be sure that it will be useful to the overall presentation. Before improvising visual aids into our speeches, the speaker should be able to know that if used incorrectly, the visual will not take its original use as an aid but will automatically become a distraction. Planning is always very important when making use of visual aids. It is paramount to choose a visual aid that foes in line for the material and audience.

The use of visual aids can be very beneficial when doing a presentation. It can really impact it if used appropriately. The purpose of the visual aid is to further enhance the presentation and not take it over.

Visual aids are not to be likened notes. Instead, they should emphasize the message and add impact to it, thus, visual aids will help to increase what listeners have remembered and how long they can retain it.

Visual elements

OBJECTS

Making use of objects as visual aids involves having to bring the actual object to demonstrate on when the speech is ongoing. For example, when giving a speech about knot tying, it is usually better to ring a tie itself.

- **Pros**: the use of actual objects is very necessary when demonstrating how to do something, this way, the audience will fully understand the procedure.
- **Cons**: some objects might be too large or unavailable for a speaker to bring along with them.

MODELS

Models are similar representations of the real object that serve as a means of demonstrating that making use of the real object is ineffective either because it is too big or because it is inaccessible.

A good example includes the use of a human skeletal system, the solar system, or architecture in a presentation.

- **Pros**: models can serve as very good substitutes that provide a better example of what the real thing is to the audience especially when the object being spoken about is of an awkwardly huge size or not available for use in the demonstration.

- **Cons**: sometimes a model might deviate from the reality of what is being presented to the audience. For example, the enormous size of the solar system cannot be effectively seen from a small model, and the actual systems of a human body cannot be seen from a dummy.

GRAPHS

Graphs are used to see the relationships between different quantities. Various types of health's are used as visual aids, and this includes line graphs, bar graphs, pie graphs, and scatter plots.

- **Pros**: graphs are used by the presenter to help the audience to see the statistics so that they can make a greater impact than just paying attention to them verbally would.
- **Cons**: graphs can easily become cluttered when being used in communication by including too many details, this can become very overwhelming for the audience and makes the graph ineffective. Thereby, persuasion will not be effective especially when trying to make the audience or listener do something you want.

MAPS

Maps are used basically to show the geographical areas that are of interest to the presentation. They most often are used as aids when speaking of differences between the geographical areas or showing the location of something.

- **Pros**: whenever maps are used simply and clearly, they can be used to properly make points about certain areas. For example, when a map shows the building site for a new hospital, it could show its very close location to key neighbourhoods around the area, or a map could also show the differences in the distribution of HIV victims in North Africa and European countries. This can aid in proper understanding.
- **Cons**: The addition of too much detail on the map may cause the audience to lose interest in the key point being made. If also the map is unrealistic or disproportional, it may become ineffective and irrelevant for the point being made thereby making the persuasion unreachable.

TABLES

Tables are rows and columns that help to organize words, symbols, and data.

- **Pros**: A very well drawn table is usually very easy to understand. Tables are a good way to compare real facts and also to gain an overall understanding of the topic that is being discussed. To illustrate, a table is a very good choice to make use of when comparing the amount of rainfall in 3 continents each month.
- **Cons**: Too many people, tables are not very interesting or really pleasing to the eye. They can be too overwhelming if the information is too much and are in small spaces or the information is not well organized in a convenient way.

It is also not a good choice to make use of if the person who is viewing it has to take a whole lot of time to be able to fully understand it. Tables can also be visual distractions if it is too hard to read because the font used is too small or the writing is probably just too close together. It can also be a means of visual distraction if the table is not drawn properly.

PHOTOGRAPHS

- **Pros**: Photographs are very good tools to make or emphasize the point effectively or to explain a topic. For example, when trying to explain the shantytowns in a Third World country it would be beneficial to show a picture of one of the towns so that the reader can get a better understanding of how those people live in their towns.
A photograph is also great to use when the actual object cannot be seen. For example, in a health class when the students are learning about cocaine, the teacher cannot bring in cocaine to the class to show the students because that would be illegal. Instead, the teacher could show them a picture of cocaine in the class. Using local photos can also help with an emphasis on how your topic is important in your audience's area of interest.
- **Cons**: If the photograph is not big, it can just become a distraction. Enlarging photographs can as well be expensive if one is not using a PowerPoint or another good viewing device.

DRAWINGS OR DIAGRAMS

- **Pros**: Drawings or diagrams can be made use of when photographs do not show exactly what it is that the speaker wants to show or explain. It could also be used if a photograph is too detailed. For example, a diagram or drawing of the circulatory system throughout the whole body is more effective than a the of a cadaver showing the circulatory system.

- **Cons**: If the picture is not drawn correctly, it can look sloppy and also be really ineffective. This type of drawing will usually appear unprofessional.

Visual aids media: simple to advanced

Over time, there has been a major improvement in what is being used to pass information across to people or to a group of people. From the ancient days of making use of sticks and soils to slates and chalk and then to black and whiteboards, we have now evolved to making use of more advanced technology in passing information to people. This has overall made things easier. As with what we have written, all visual aids of passing information have their own advantages and disadvantages too. We need to learn how to make use of them and remember that the visual aids are meant to be complementary and not substitutional.

The new aids are more subject to issues relating to distraction and that is why most times, placards are usually where there are either prints or drawings. As for photographs, they seem to make the audience change course from the point being passed. One of the big advantages of using the advanced means of visual aids is that one is able to make the presentation without the need of another person or people. Using slides on a projector is a big example. Instead of having people carry photographs, drawings or placards with prints, one can easily use a remote of control what is being presented by sliding through every time they want new content. This means however that everything will need to be pre-arranged before the day of the speech or presentation using a computer.

A disadvantage of this is that the audience can easily be distracted compared to using the other old ways of padding information. Another disadvantage is that it is really expensive to get proper visual aids of this type and so many presenters who do not have that in their budget will prefer to get aids that are cheaper and try to make the best out of it. It is hard to choose for anyone which type of visual aid they should use as this is totally based on preference. Some people who do not have enough will choose to use the old types of aids and some prefer the advanced ones.

The one to be used can also be dependent on what you want from the presentation. If the presentation is meant to be amusing for example with a kind of informal setting, it is usually more advisable to make use of visual and audio that will arouse their urge to go on. In most cases, this will be making use of placards, drawings, graphs and pictures. The advanced use of this aids, however, can be used mostly in formal settings.

This type is what most people make use in contract proposal presentation or sales pitches. They are also used in conferences and public addresses or political campaigns.

The use of visual aids has moved from being simple to getting advanced and every day, more are being brought up to help the audience understand what is being presented thereby bring the chances of persuasion into possibility. We will look here at the simple and the advanced use of visual aids going how they have developed.

Chalkboard or whiteboard

These are no longer as popular as they used to some years ago especially with the blackboard. The whiteboard is still used up to today and they are usually called the magic boards in the past. Chalkboards and whiteboards are visual aids that have been very useful, particularly when the advanced types of media are not available. They are also very cheap, and they also allow for flexibility.

The use of this type of visual aid is convenient, but as stated before, they are not a perfect visual aid. Not times, making use of this medium as an aid might create a type of confusion or boredom in communication. When for example, a student who is not familiar with how to effectively use visual aids is asked to draw on a board while they are speaking, they detract time and attention from their real speech.

Poster board

A poster is a very simple to use and easy to understand visual aid.

Posters can display pictures, charts, graphs, or illustrations. One of the major drawbacks of using a poster as a means of visual aid in trying to persuade an audience is that often, a poster can appear very unprofessional. Since a poster board paper is mostly flimsy, often the paper might bend or fall over if being held up. To get the best out of using a poster, it is advisable to hang it up or tape it to a wall. They are also known as placards.

Handouts

The use of Handouts can be very helpful to the presenter because they can easily follow up what is going on or what the presenter is saying using the aid of the hand-out. The hand-outs can display graphs, charts, pictures, or illustrations. An important aspect of making use of a hand-out is that the audience can keep a hand-out with them even after the presentation is over. This can help the person to remember what was discussed in the course of the presentation. However, passing out hand-outs can be a big genesis of distraction. Once a hand-out is shared amongst them, it might usually very difficult to bring back the audience's attention.

The person who has received the hand-out might be tempted to only read what is written on the paper, which will stop them from listening to exactly what the speaker is saying. If using a hand-out, it is usually very advisable that the speaker distributes all the handout before the start of the whole presentation or better still before the presenter references the hand-out.

Usually in a lecture that will span for about an hour or maybe two hours, distributing hand-outs is acceptable, but in short lectures of five to ten minutes, a hand-out is not very advisable as the time will not be enough for the students to check out the hand-out. In this case, it will be better that the lecturer reads everything to the students from the hand-out so that they do not lose focus.

Video excerpts

A short video can as well be a good visual aid and attention grabber when communicating. However, a video should not be a replacement for an actual speech. For playing a video in a presentation or in class, there are several potential drawbacks.

Firstly, if the video that is playing includes audio, then the speaker will not be able to talk, and this has already taken the while floor from the presenter.

Secondly, if the video being played is very exciting and interesting too, it will then make the speaker appear rather boring and uninteresting. This will draw away the interest of the listeners and they will start to do other things to talking to one another of the concluded video. To best make things better and to have a good video presentation without making your audience lose interest in what is being said, it is better that the presenter makes use of shorter videos and also make sure that the speech is being transitioned into the videos as well. This way, everything will go smoothly.

Projection equipment

In today's world, there are many different types of projectors. These include PowerPoint presentations, slide projectors, computer projectors, and overhead projectors. Slide projectors are the oldest form of the projector on this list. They are rarely ever used again. PowerPoint presentations, on the other hand, are very popular and are still used very often.

Overhead projectors are still fairly used around the globe and this is because they are inconvenient to use. To better use an overhead projector, a sort of transparency must be made of whatever the presenter wants to project onto the screen. This can take a lot of time and costs lots of money.

Computer projectors are the most technologically advanced projectors of everyone in this list. When making use of a computer projector, pictures and slides can easily be taken right from the computer either online or from a saved file already on the computer and are blown up and shown on a bigger screen. Though they are technologically advanced and very easy to use as well, they are not usually completely reliable because technological breakdowns are very common on the computers of today.

Computer-assisted presentations

PowerPoint presentations can be an extremely important visual aid, especially for presentations that will last for longer periods. If the presentation is not going to be long or if it is going to take less than ten minutes, then it is probably not worth the time or effort to use a powerpoint. For longer presentations, however, PowerPoints can be a great way to keep the audience glued and also to keep the speaker on track.

A potential downside of using a PowerPoint is that it in most cases usually takes a lot of time and energy to start it up. There is also the already mentioned possibility of the computer malfunctioning, which can mess up the complete balance of a presentation.

Social media

One of the most effective ways to communicate is to make use of social media. For a few years now, people have been able to meet with people. Get deals done, persuade others and also start a war using social media.

Using the platform, people have been made and people have been broken. Over the years, the use of social media has widened and new ways to communicate on the platform has been developed which makes the use of images, audio and also videos. The adoption of text and images has been able to help deliver messages quicker and more easily through social media platforms.

A big drawback to using social media is that there is very limited access for some people due to the requirements of internet access and other certain limitations to the number of characters and image size depending mainly on the platform being used.

COMMUNICATION BARRIERS TO PERSUASION

There are many barriers to effective persuasion in the process of communicating the information and this can retard or distort the content or motive of the information the persuader wants to convey. These barriers often lead to failure in the persuasive stages or undesirable outcomes. These include political correctness, selective perception, emotions, language, silence, filtering, communication apprehension, information overload, gender differences and so on.

This might also include a lack of expressing appropriate knowledge intended as it usually happens when a person make use of ambiguous legal terminologies, medical registers, or descriptions that are not well understood by the audience.

- **Physical barriers**: These are units which are often related to the atmosphere of the setting. For example, natural barrier is a type of barrier often associated with this where one can see if employees are found in completely different sites or found in different buildings. Also, poor equipment or out-dated ones, especially the failure coming from the governing body to introduce a new system of technology, might be another reason for major problems. The shortage of employees is another issue which can often reduce the effectiveness of communication in a company.

- **System design**: Another barrier to effective communication is system design which deals with the issues in the system or structure of an organisation's existence. Examples could be the structure of the organisation which, in most cases, is not straightforward. Hence, identifying who to commune with is often difficult. The other major examples are inappropriate or inefficient communication system, inefficiency in supervision and not clearly stating roles for employees as these can ultimately lead to the employees not knowing exactly what is demanded of them to do while at work.

- **Attitudinal barriers**: These spring up in correlation to issues among staffs in any organization of people. These may be a result of poor management, personal interests or personal beefs which may invariably result in people unwilling to communicate among one another.

Also, when employees lose motivations to work or they are dissatisfied towards a particular task which proper training was not provided for, they engage in the act of giving attitudes to individuals or to the employers and as such, to communicate would become too difficult to achieve.

- **Ambiguity in utterances**: often, some words have the same pronunciation but with different meaning and the use of these words would lead to ambiguity in communication because the decoder might find it difficult to decipher what the encoder is passing across as message.

The encoder must then ensure that they make the decoder get the right message to ensure that meaning is passed successfully by reducing the use of ambiguous words.

- **Individual linguistic ability**: Idiolects is language-use that is peculiar to individuals. The use of jargons, slangs and inappropriate words during communication can prevent the decoder from understanding what the encoder is passing across. Messages that are not understood can cause confusion and researches have pointed out that confusion can add legitimacy to a research even when persuasion fails.

- **Bypassing**: This barrier happens when both communicators (sender and the receiver) do not give the same symbolic meaning to the words they speak. It is when the encoder is trying to communicate but the decoder is getting a different meaning to whatever the sender is passing across. For example- Restroom, ASAP etc.

- **Technological multi-tasking and absorbency**: With the constant increment in the level of technologically oriented modes of communication in the past few decades, many individuals are increasingly being made to face with communication in forms of text, emails and social updates.

In turn, this has led to a visible change in the way the younger generation has been able to communicate and see their own self-efficacy to connect and communicate with others. With the constant presence of new worlds in a person's hand, people have started multi-tasking both physically and cognitively as a constant reminder of something else that is already happening somewhere else can bombard them. Though perhaps this is too new of advancement to yet be able to see long-term effects, this is a notion currently explored by many scholars.

- **Fear of being criticized**: This is one major factor that stops good communication. If we are to exercise simple practices to help improve our communication skill, we will see that we can really become better communicators. For example, if you read an article that is written in a newspaper or you collect some news from listening to the television and do a presentation of it in front of the mirror, this will not only help boost your confidence but will also improve your language and your vocabulary.

- **Gender barriers**: Most communicators whether they are aware or not do often have a certain agenda of theirs. Amongst the different type of genders, this is very notable. For example, in our world, many women have been found to do more critical thinking when it comes to addressing conflict.

It's also been researched that men are more than likely to draw out from conflict when compared to women. This comparison and breakdown have not only shown that there are plenty of factors to consider in communication between two genders but there is also room for improvement and established guidelines for all.

PERSUASION AND BUSINESS

Persuasion is a very important aspect of a business. It is, in fact, the basis of any business and therefore anyone who wants to go into any kind of business must be it online or a stall or own a company generally should learn all the rudiments of communicative persuasion.

Persuasion as a concept is evident in every form of communication and that is why it was stated earlier in this discourse that everyone at a point in their lives must have made use of persuasion. To drive effective business communication, persuasion is needed. Without properly understanding how to use persuasion, the business owner might fall short of customers and find it hard to win people over to his ideas. Here's a list of those that might need to use persuasion in business.

The owner of a small or big business trying to get a customer:

- A person or a company trying to get a contract
- A staff who wants to win a sales pitch
- An employee

- A company who is into media and wants to advertise a product to specific people
- Finally, a customer.

The final party on the list of who will want to use persuasion in business here might come as a bit of a surprise but there are bargains in every business and so during the course of any bargain, the customer also tries the convenience the seller that the price should be brought down to the convenience of both parties.

The question now is *how to persuade a person to agree with a person in the business.*

A. **Understand your audience**: The audience is not necessarily large of people; it could also be a single person or a group of people. One of the most crucial parts of any type of communication is knowing the audience and understanding them. This same criticality is also evident in business persuasion. Those who own a business must be very wary of those who they are passing information to whether an individual or a group of individuals. You have to know what they expect, what they want and what the outcome will be for what is intended. In a nutshell, you need to know what their objective is for the business.

An example is when an employee that wants to go for a conference and is looking to take permission from a boss might only be interested in the issue of the budget. The employee can make the boss see reasons why information from that conference will be beneficial for the conference but first, the employee will have to analyse the bosses' interest to help the employee better his communication with the right persuasive messages.

Another example is when a businessman is looking to sell a product, you should know exactly why your customer will like to buy your product and how it will be beneficial to your customer. By making these findings, the approach will be easier, and this will bring us to the next step.

B. **Choosing the right medium**: After knowing your audience and seeing what their interest is, it is also very important to analyse what medium of communication they would prefer. Trying to tell a boss about your absence from work over the phone will not be a good idea. The way people want to get messages really differ and some customers are prone to being convinced to get things in different ways. There is a saying that one should never quit a job over the phone. This is true because it is the wrong medium of communication based on the situation.

An example is when you want to stop to meet with a colleague unexpectedly to discuss a very vital issue. It is only agreeable if the colleague is fine by it. If not, then an email should be first put forward or preferably a call based on what the other colleague wants. In essence, for proper persuasive communication, it is vital to make use of a medium that is very appropriate both to the message being passed and to audiences' preference.

C. **Taking time to listen**: Passing information is not a way thing. When communicating to yourself, you are only telling yourself what it is that you already know. When trying to persuade another party, it is very advisable that one pays close attention to what the person is also saying. This way, you will understand that a person's emotional state and also have the power to make use of it to get what you want.

In most types of communication, it is usually a two-way thing, and this is the most effective way to persuade your audience. Often, communicators are so focused on what they want that they fail to understand the point of view or the emotional state of the audience. They do not take time to listen. As much as trying to speak is important in persuasion, listening is also important. This can help one understand the audiences' desires, motivation, interest and concerns. What we have tried to explain here is that as much as you would like to get your communication goal, it is also very important to sit back and listen to your audience.

D. **Building a strong relationship**: Having good communication is also bent towards a strong relationship. You cannot persuade a boss without having a good relationship with the boss.

You cannot persuade an audience or a customer without first building a good relationship. It is on the foundation of a good relationship that both the business owner and the customer or a colleague and another colleague can get to communicate better. Through strong relationships, regularity is ensured in business. With whoever we have built a solid and strong relationship with, we can share even our most sensitive issues. We can pass information and get feedback from them. Taking time to groom and build connections even before trying to persuade will make a significant difference in your success with persuading. An example is when an employee is trying to get persuade a boss but has a record of always coming late to work or lateness in the submission of jobs. It's easy to guess that the boss will likely not accept the proposal. This is because the employee has not left himself a good impression or building a good reputation with the boss.

Having known what to do when one wants to persuade, it is very important to state that for entrepreneurs, persuasion is a tool that is used to help get new clients, get a good worker and general move the business to a better level. People who know how to persuade are influential and people like then. They are usually the quiet ones in the room. They speak less and they eventually do, they make sense and are able to make people do things. They also make sure to put the needs of others above theirs. Here are habits of a good persuasive businessperson.

E. Curiosity and listening: As stated in how to persuade people in a business, one should have the habit to listen to effectively persuade another person. You would need to know what others want on both an emotional and also on a physical level. You should make sure to ask good questions and also listen when the person is speaking. You should be open-ended and begin discussions of this sort. You should demonstrate a genuine interest in what others do. If you can understand others by listening, persuasion will come easy. When you want to know and you are attentive, you have automatically sent a message that you value the person. With time, a reputation of trustworthiness will grow, and this is a great quality will grow.

F. Honesty: Honesty is normally a quality that s required in any business to for that business to be successful. In essence, for a business to thrive, it has to have its benchmark on transparency. This also goes for anyone who is looking to persuade in business. Your credibility and ability to persuade is dependent on your being able to be very honest in all situations. Dishonesty is very destructive and is capable of misleading others. An intentional lie can ruin your professional reputation. It is true that the truth might sometimes hurt but it is better, to be honest than to lose peoples trust due to dishonesty.

G. **Confidence**: Be it a customer, a client or a colleague, you should learn to be confident. The place of confidence cannot be side-lined in business. You should know how to show that you really believe in your ideas and in your proposal. You should also be confident in what you are selling.

Being confident when showing a product will convince a potential customer that what you have to offer is truly effective. To avoid anxiety or even self-doubt, you should remain calm when presenting anything. Also, straightforwardness should be used, do not dabble about the whole thing. State your position and validate it with clear factual points.

H. **Effective voicing**: Once you have said something, people will begin to make decisions based on the way you have communicated with them. You do not need to be scared or begin to murmur. When communicating, it is advisable to speak slowly and also know when you're speaking slowly so that you can raise your voice to speak loudly but still clearly. Making use of brief pauses will make being clear easier. Emphasize your points better and avoid fillers like uh.

I. Tell a story: People will enjoy your speech better when you are able to chip in a story. A well-told story should be enjoyable ad be themed towards what you have to offer. Stories have the ability to persuade others in the business. It is always good to move away from the stress of business to tell a good story. As opposed to facts, the way people pay attention differs. Your story must be able to make a connection between what the client is thinking and what they are already thinking, what the client believes and what you intend him to believe.